ROBERT'S DAY OF EMOTIONS & HALLOWEEN

ROBERT'S DAY OF EMOTIONS & HALLOWEEN

PRINCE ALBERT KING

Little story about big feelings

PRINCE KING DIGITAL PRINTING (PKDP) PRESS

By Prince Albert King (Author), PKDP (Illustrator)

Help your child self-regulate their emotions. Roberts' Day of Emotions Books: A Little Story about BIG Feelings teaches emotional control and how to effectively act when faced with overwhelming emotions or challenging circumstances. The book has a twist at the end with a door to door treat or treat story.

ROBERTS' DAY OF EMOTIONS & HALLOWEEN

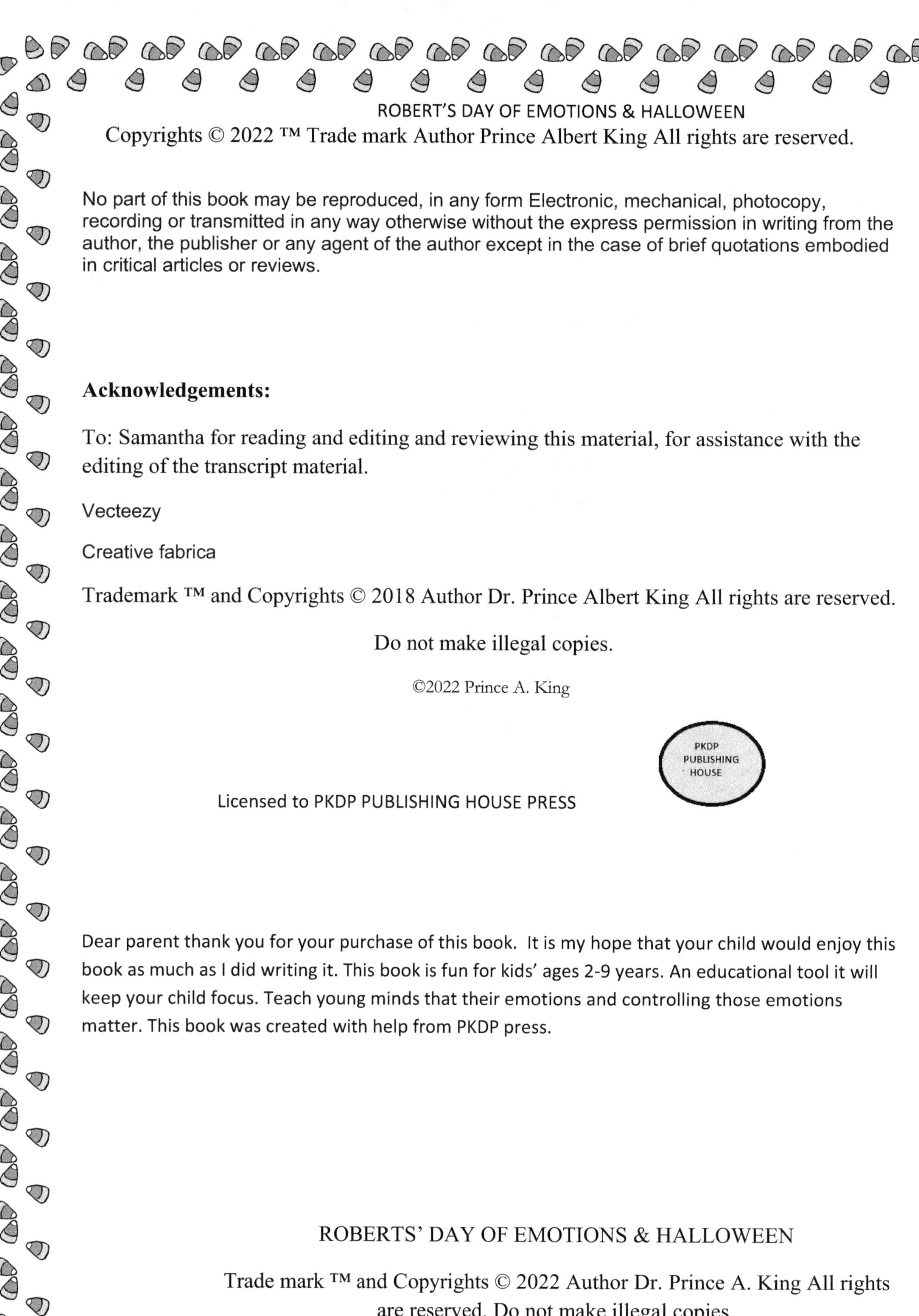

Acknowledgements:

To: Samantha for reading and editing and reviewing this material, for assistance with the editing of the transcript material.

Vecteezy

Creative fabrica

Licensed to PKDP PUBLISHING HOUSE PRESS

PKDP PUBLISHING HOUSE

Dear parent thank you for your purchase of this book. It is my hope that your child would enjoy this book as much as I did writing it. This book is fun for kids' ages 2-9 years. An educational tool it will keep your child focus. Teach young minds that their emotions and controlling those emotions matter. This book was created with help from PKDP press.

ROBERTS' DAY OF EMOTIONS & HALLOWEEN

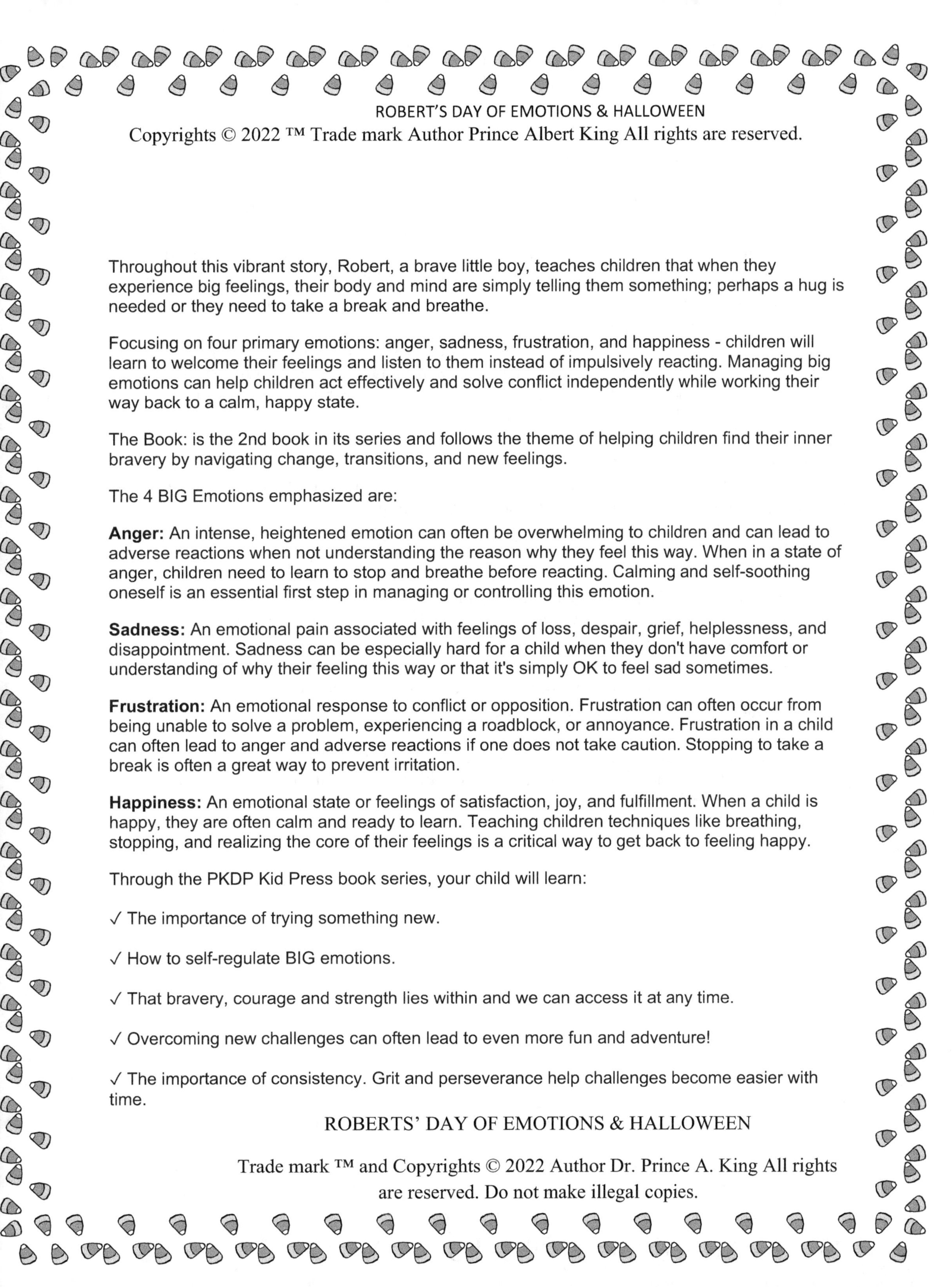

ROBERT'S DAY OF EMOTIONS & HALLOWEEN

Throughout this vibrant story, Robert, a brave little boy, teaches children that when they experience big feelings, their body and mind are simply telling them something; perhaps a hug is needed or they need to take a break and breathe.

Focusing on four primary emotions: anger, sadness, frustration, and happiness - children will learn to welcome their feelings and listen to them instead of impulsively reacting. Managing big emotions can help children act effectively and solve conflict independently while working their way back to a calm, happy state.

The Book: is the 2nd book in its series and follows the theme of helping children find their inner bravery by navigating change, transitions, and new feelings.

The 4 BIG Emotions emphasized are:

Anger: An intense, heightened emotion can often be overwhelming to children and can lead to adverse reactions when not understanding the reason why they feel this way. When in a state of anger, children need to learn to stop and breathe before reacting. Calming and self-soothing oneself is an essential first step in managing or controlling this emotion.

Sadness: An emotional pain associated with feelings of loss, despair, grief, helplessness, and disappointment. Sadness can be especially hard for a child when they don't have comfort or understanding of why their feeling this way or that it's simply OK to feel sad sometimes.

Frustration: An emotional response to conflict or opposition. Frustration can often occur from being unable to solve a problem, experiencing a roadblock, or annoyance. Frustration in a child can often lead to anger and adverse reactions if one does not take caution. Stopping to take a break is often a great way to prevent irritation.

Happiness: An emotional state or feelings of satisfaction, joy, and fulfillment. When a child is happy, they are often calm and ready to learn. Teaching children techniques like breathing, stopping, and realizing the core of their feelings is a critical way to get back to feeling happy.

Through the PKDP Kid Press book series, your child will learn:

✓ The importance of trying something new.

✓ How to self-regulate BIG emotions.

✓ That bravery, courage and strength lies within and we can access it at any time.

✓ Overcoming new challenges can often lead to even more fun and adventure!

✓ The importance of consistency. Grit and perseverance help challenges become easier with time.

ROBERTS' DAY OF EMOTIONS & HALLOWEEN

✓ The incredible feeling of conquering hard things!

✓ That kindness always wins.

ROBERTS DAY OF EMOTIONS AND HALLOWEEN

Help your child self-regulate their emotions. Roberts' Day of Emotions Books: A Little Story about BIG Feelings teaches emotional control and how to effectively act when faced with overwhelming emotions or challenging circumstances. The book has a twist at the end with a door to door treat or treat story.

From the Author: Dear parent thank you for your purchase of this book. It is my hope that your child would enjoy this book as much as I did writing it. This book is fun for kids' ages 3-9 years. An educational tool it will keep your child focus. Teach young minds that their emotions and controlling those emotions matter.

When children are angry, they can manifest their anger through bad behavior. They might shout, cry, throw things and roll on the floor or all of these things combined. That's why most parents need help managing their kids emotions and feelings.

This book about little Robert:

- contains lovely illustrations and a storyline
- helps children recognize and cope with their anger in a real way through communication of positive affirmations.
- offers a calming technique and is aimed to improve kids self-regulation skills
- teaches children to admit their mistakes. forgive others and say "I'm sorry"
- includes a bonus coloring page

"This story will help preschoolers to understand, recognize and deal with their emotions. Very useful picture book which offers fun kids activities and has illustrations. This book was created with help from PKDP press.

ROBERTS' DAY OF EMOTIONS & HALLOWEEN

Table of contents

Chapter 1 The Night Mare

Chapter 2 Facing Fear

Chapter3 Feeling Sad

Chapter4 Facing Anger

Chapter5 It Feels Good To Be Happy

Chapter6 Trick or treat

ROBERTS' DAY OF EMOTIONS & HALLOWEEN

Chapter 1 The Night Mare

Robert had been watching some movies (The night mare on Elm Street) and Hocus Pocus about Halloween before going to bed. Afterwards he was told by mom to go to sleep. "Sleep is very important, for the mind to rest" she said. Robert said" Good night" and went to sleep peacefully. While in a deep sleep, Robert began to have a nightmare.

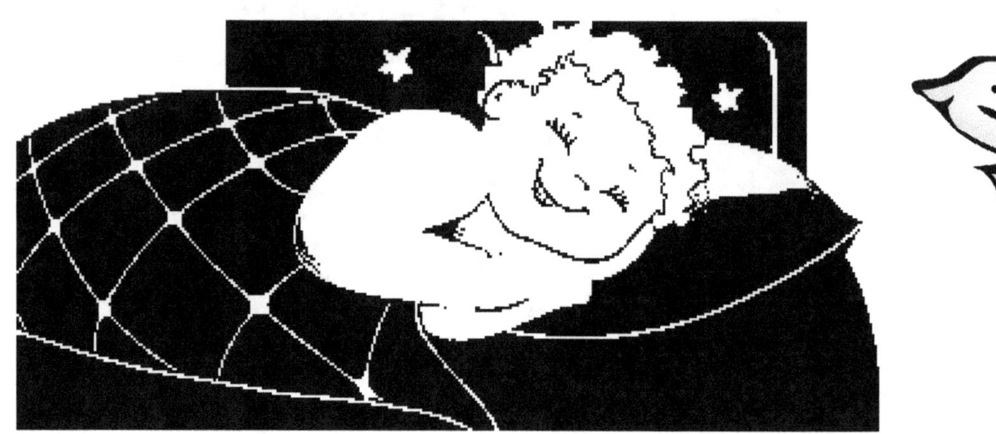

It was a beautiful morning Only Robert did not know how beautiful it was yet. Because he had jump up out of bed having been awaken from a nightmare, after dreaming about Halloween.

Halloween is tomorrow Robert said to himself. He was frightened so, He got up and ran to his dad.

"I'm scared" He said to dad. "Why are you Scared?" Dad replied.

"I'm scared because I had a night mare, the Halloween ghost and monsters were chasing me, and the pumpkins were all laughing at me"

Ha,Ha,Ha,

"Watching horror movies and eating too much pizza can cause you to have nightmares" dad said. Dad continued "Fear comes upon everyone at some time in our lives. We must face our fears to overcome them". "You are stronger than fear." Robert did not know this yet, but lessons come in each situation. But we have to learn from those lessons.

Dad said "Say it! Robert" I AM STRONGER THAN MY FEARS." "Two more times with more power!"

STOP BREATHE REWIND

Take a deep, breath then exhale slowly, breathe then exhale, breathe slowly, then exhale... It's only a dream". It is not real, Calm so down".

Do you know what imagination is son? He asked. "Yes dad" said the boy." Like thinking about things in picture form". " Dad said" It is the ability to form a picture in your mind's eye of something that doesn't exist, has not yet happened, or that one has not experienced.

'You can control your imagination just like you can control your emotions and thoughts by doing something new "Dad held Robert in his arms it's not real" Dad said.

Stop, think and listen to your heart and eyes" have you ever seen this in real life? Robert started to think No dad" he replied. Then "every time you have a bad dream, stop where you are and say" I will not accept this dream, I refuse it". Then breathe a few times. You can use your imagination to change the channel in your mind to think on true, pure and good things. Form a picture in your mind's eye of something that has happened, or that you want to see, enjoy or experience.

Robert Had forgotten that before going to bed, that he had been watching television about werewolves, witches and monsters. Maybe the images were still in his subs conscience during his sleep.

Start to think on good things like your last birthday party, playing with friends and family trips." You know like the time we went to Disney land for your first time".

They both started to laugh, just thinking of all the fun the family had. Robert was not scared any more, He said" next time Dad I will be brave and fight the fear.

The next day Robert awoke to have a good day the sun was shining bright.

ROBERTS' DAY OF EMOTIONS & HALLOWEEN

His sister told him about the fun she had last year on Halloween night during the treat or treat walk in the neighborhood. Lots of candy. Robert loved candy.

He couldn't wait for the candy bag to see all the goodies inside.

Chapter 2 Feeling Sad

That day Robert's elder brother Charlie being the naughty annoying older brother as older brothers do, came into Robert's room while he was playing and took his toy dinosaur away and ran with it.

Robert began to cry. The tears fell from his eyes and flowed for a while He was sad. Emotions began to run wild.

Have you ever been sad? Of course you have. Everyone gets sad from time to time Tears come when we are sad. But we can change our thoughts from sadness to happy thoughts.

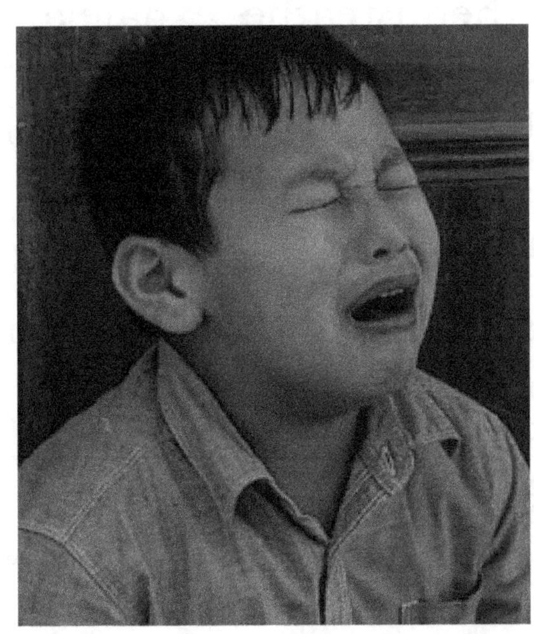

Chapter 3 Facing Anger

Then He became angry and frustrated, He felt like screaming and picking up something and throwing it at his brother. He shouted "bring it back you big bully" Robert was frustrated because he couldn't do anything about it. He felt helpless because mom and dad were not at time at the time. They had gone out to get Halloween supplies for the evening event. Then He heard Dad's Voice in his head" remember when bad things happen; First you stop, and Say" I'm Stronger than Anger" Breathe a few times and think of doing something different or imagine nice things that happen in the past. Robert Breathe and exhaled, then Breathe, exhale and he breathe. The more he breathe it got easier then better and better until He calmed Himself down while lying in his bed. He was now back to normal. He smiled "Dad would be proud of me" He said.

After a while Charlie who had expected Robert to come running after him in a rage as usual returned to the room with the toy, very disappointed. He said "you're no fun, any more Robert!" "I forgive you for all the times that you took my toys, Charlie you cannot make me mad anymore." What's gotten into you? Who are you? Where is my brother?" Charlie said as he left the room.

Dinosaur

Chapter 4 Facing Frustration

"Kindness always wins". Mom had said that. Robert knew that he had conquered being able to take his brother, Charlie's annoying behavior. He saw for the first time in his life that by controlling his feelings He caused Charlie not to be in control of them and that Charlie was no longer the puppet master. Robert felt free it was not as hard as he had taught all along, He was in complete control it was fun to see Charlie's facial expression. Never again would he let Charlie make him sweat. He had control inside him and he could always reach inside and pull it out, in any given situation or at any time. He was really stronger than Anger today, but he still had many more times in life to practice controlling his emotions.

Chapter5 It Feels Good To Be Happy

Finally mom and dad returned home. Robert related the events of his day so far to them. Everyone gets scare, angry, sad and frustrated at some time." You are brave, strong and fearless" dad said. "Only you can give someone permission to control your emotions". "Just do not give it to them and you will stay in control. You are in control of your mind and body. Make it obey your wishes." Continue to change your thoughts to something new it's like changing the channel on the television". "Imagine being on the beach in the sand feeling the cool breeze blowing peacefully. Or laying down looking at the starry sky at night and finding the big dipper".

Mom reach out her hands to him. "I think someone needs a hug, give me some sugar" She said.

It's good to be happy, said Robert.

Chapter 6 Trick or Treat

Dad called Charlie and Dannell into the room. You are to prepare for tonight's festivities, He said.

"Everyone try on your costumes please". It was time for trick or treat. Robert was dressed as a ghost. The kids went from door to door with their parents to guide them to collect their candy treats.

When the children got to the next house, they were unaware or the argument that the couple had just had before their arrival. George never wanted kids and so he was always annoyed at Halloween when kids came knowing at door. George loved candy and so he was like an Ebenezer scrooge on Halloween day. Candy was like gold to him from him was a child. He hoarded it at every chance he got. Samantha had saved the candy for the children a wek before when she shopped. Upon checking that day she had discovered that, someone had been in the cookie jar,she knew that someone had to be George." George where is the candies for the children? "I only took some of them, He said with an evil smile on his face. Come on it is Halloween after all what is a little treat without a trick to? Suddenly there was the dreaded knock on the door that the couple both had anticipated and the shouts of...

"Trick-or-treat!" the children outside yelled in unison, their greedy hands already reaching out for candy and cookies hoping they would get something nice. She forced a smile. Reached out and repeatedly said "Here you go," as she gave each child, dispersing among them a meager share of candy. She wanted to give them more, but she had to conserve the little bit that remained after her husband got through with the cookie jar. The werewolf glared at her like she was the candy, and the little Ghost looked surprised making up his face in horror, but they accepted it, mumbled some thanks, and walked away on their quest to rob the next house of the candy gold..

She shut the door, leaned against it, and stared at what was left of the candy. It wasn't enough. Not nearly enough. What was she to do? Panicking internally, she rushed into the kitchen and started pulling ingredients off the pantry shelves, practically flinging them onto the counter.

"What's gotten into you? What are you doing?

"George questioned, appearing in the doorway.

"What's it look like I'm doing? I'm making cookies and candy. Just leave me to it! I need quiet," she snapped, not glancing up as she dug through the spice shelf looking for the vanilla extract. Not finding it immediately, she began to fling plastic spice jars to the floor as she searched. The vanilla extract bottle rolled across the kitchen counter and fell to George's feet, and he bent down to retrieve it.

"Trick-or-treat!" the children outside yelled in unison, their greedy hands already reaching out for goodies. She forced a smile. "Here you go," she said, dispersing among them a meager share of candy. She wanted to give them more, but she had to conserve the little bit that remained after her husband got through with the bag. The werewolf glared at her like she was dinner, and Goldilocks made a face like the porridge was too hot, but they accepted it, mumbled some thanks, and walked away.

She shut the door, leaned against it, and stared at what was left of the candy. It wasn't enough. Not nearly enough. Panicking internally, she rushed into the kitchen and started pulling ingredients off the pantry shelves, practically flinging them onto the counter along with her mother’s recipe for home-made candy.

"What the heaven's gotten into you? What are you doing now?" George questioned, appearing in the doorway.

"What's it look like I'm doing? I'm making cookies. Just leave me alone," she snapped, not glancing up as she dug through the spice shelf looking for ginger. Not finding it immediately, she began to fling plastic spice jars to the floor as she searched. One of these rolled across the kitchen to George's feet, and he bent down to retrieve it.

I must get this done before the next set of children arrives but it will take at least forty-five minutes. George hearing this decided to cut off the lights out side and in the front room to appear that on one was home." it will buy us sometime" he said. There was a wicked smile on his face as he grinned to himself, throwing himself into the Halloween mood of playing the trickster while his wife gave the treats. Janet did not hear him she kept on baking the cookies. George had hoped to leave the lights off intentionally hoping all the children would pass the house by so that eventually all of the goodies would be for himself. He secretly planned to place a raw egg into each bag that she wife had planned to give each child as part of his trick after she had filled each bag, He would personally volunteer his services helping to seal each bag and his wife would not be the wiser. He remembered his old neighbor Ms. Daisy who he had believed to be a witch playing the same trick on him as a teen only her eggs very much prepared weeks before Halloween and spoiled to the core. She did give good candies but she liked to add the trick with the treat. Once he confronted her about it and she replied, "why son? He was now an adult and realized that Ms. Daisy was only having fun with the kids. But boy she looked and act out the part, dressed as a witch in that witches hat with the makeup and all, she replied" You know sonny; to keep up the tradition! Then she would put an evil grin on her face. This made George frustrated, so the next year he took revenge by dressing in his costume and covering her front porch in rotten eggs. His neighbor had done this to all of the children in the neighborhood over the years, so she never knew which child did the trick with the rotten eggs on her." Well Ms. Daisy is no longer with us so the tradition must be carried out only I will use good eggs this time he said. "Yes, it will honor her memory. George threw his head back and began to laugh with glee; ha-ha, ha-ha, it was so delightful. What a Halloween scrooge.

Janet was surprised to see that George had changed into the Dracula costume that she had brought for him a year before. He had in his own words" refused to be a part of Halloween because of past experiences "he had told her. Now he was lightening up. She always taught that he was to stiff, not able to take jokes sometimes. "Wow honey you really have thrown yourself into the season all of a sudden" she said. "I feel like having a little fun with the kids "He said. Really, are you ok? She questioned." I'm fine. "As a measure of good will, I'll help you pack and seal the bags too from now on" he said." Wow that would help me save time; time is of the essence right now" she said. "I got this." He said. George was still holding on to his hidden agenda;.

The time had passed. The timer rang out.

Just in time for Janet to notice that the front porch light was off." Honey did you turn off the lights? "Yes dear." To buy you more time! He shouted after her from the kitchen. He had filled each bag, and started to walk towards the front room.

Janet flicked up the light switch, the children saw the light and approached the house porch.

Robert, Charles and Dannell arrived to the door." Trick or Treat "Welcome here you go" said George Treats for you and you and you" Thank you the children said in unison. By now Robert and his siblings had a cart load of goodies. Their costumes looked so realistic. Robert in his ghost costume, Dannell dress as a witch and Charles as a werewolf. It was time to go home now. Dad said "to the car kids!" and off they went. Upon arrival home, while in his room Robert began counting his loot. To his surprise he had an Egg. This made him a little puzzle I wonder why an egg was inside. He later discovered that Dannell and Charlie's bag also had an Egg. Each child took out the egg and gave it to mom after related the story of the evening's activities. Mom and dad taught it strange too. Can you tell which house gave the egg? Mom asked." We did go trick –o- treating "said Robert.

Everyone got it except dad at first. Then Mom said" hon, It was not a treat!" "Oh It's a Trick" Dad finally figured it out, It was a trick with a treat. "Ohm, like dah Dad" the children said in unison"

Everyone began to laugh and they laughed. The end.

In remembrance of Daisy

Trick -o -treat

PKDP PRESS Nassau,N.P. Bahamas.

Other works - Books by this Author – Prince Albert King

Chickcharnee Forest

Nothing for Christmas

Violet

The Johnnycake Man

The Chickcharnee Prince

The Doll

My first toddler coloring book

Nothing for Christmas 2

Pkdp Christmas children's activity coloring book

Ocean and sea animal coloring book

Roberts Day of Emotions

Chickcharney Wars

Vieola

The treasure coast a tale of pirates

The Christmas story coloring activity book

ABC Animal Activity Coloring book

And many more.

Available in paperback format.

ROBERTS' DAY OF EMOTIONS & HALLOWEEN

HALLOWEEN ACTIVITIES

Color the pictures below:

Bat

Treat bag

Goodie bag

Color the pictures

Candy

COLOR THE WORDS AND THE WEREWOLF WHAT EVER YOU LIKE

HI I AM FRANKENSTEIN

COLOR THE BODY OF FRANKIE BROWN

COLOR FRANKIE'S COAT GREEN

PRINTABLE ACTIVITY SHEET

LOOK THEN CREATE A SENTENCE USING THE PICTURES

ACTIVITY 1.

MY NAME IS: …………………………………………..

THE CANDY CORN IS____________________

SWEET	CORN	IS THE	CANDY

ANS.SWEET

ACTIVITY 2.

THE _________ APPLES ARE SO ______________

APPLE	SWEET	CANDY	ARE SO

MY NAME IS: …………………………………………..

ANS.: I CANDY 2. SWEET

COLOR THE VAMPIRE:

FACE BROWN:

CAPE RED

COAT BLACK

PANTS & SHOES BLACK

CAN YOU HELP FRANKIE TO FIND HIS HEAD, AND KEEP HIS COOL?

COLOR THE MAZE

HELP THE SEEDS TO GET TO THE APPLES

FACTS AND TRADITION OF TRICK- O- TREAT (HALLOWEEN)

The practice can be traced to the ancient Celts, early Roman Catholics and The 17th-century British. Trick-or-treating—setting off on Halloween night in costume and ringing doorbells to demand treats—has been a tradition in the United States and other countries for more than a century.

WHY DO WE SAY TRICK OR TREAT?

The phrase makes **a suggestion that if a treat (like candy) is given, then the child will not perform a "trick" (mischief) on the owner of the house**.

What is the true meaning of Halloween?

"Hallow" — or holy person — refers to the saints celebrated on All Saints' Day, which is November 1. The "een" part of the word is a contraction of "eve" — or evening before. So basically, Halloween is just an old-fashioned way of saying "**the night before All Saints' Day**" — also called Hallowmas or All Hallows' Day.

Why do we give out candy on Halloween?

While the candy industry was on the hunt for a fall holiday, neighborhood parents were looking for an organized activity **to keep youngsters out of trouble**. And by the late 1940s, passing out treats was established as an alternative to tricks.

For booking events – book signings contact:

PKDP PUBLISHING PRESS.

P.O.BOX SB51712 NASSAU N.P., BAHAMAS

Email: https://www.authorpaking@gmail.com

https://www.pkdpsales@gmail.com

ROBERTS' DAY OF EMOTIONS & HALLOWEEN

ABOUT THE AUTHOR

Prince Albert King lives in Nassau, Bahamas. He is married to the beautiful Samantha Wilson King. The couple has four children. He is a history buff and a third generation Retired Police Officer. Prince is also a Computer Technician and Website designer.

Printed in the United States Of America.

www.ingramcontent.com/pod-product-compliance
Lightning Source LLC
LaVergne TN
LVHW080558160826
845677LV00010B/1903
* 9 7 9 8 3 5 7 9 2 3 2 9 5 *